CW00687591

stories & souls

WRITTEN AND PHOTOGRAPHED BY HANNISZE

IN MEMORY OF MY PARENTS,
WHO TAUGHT ME TO LIVE, LOVE, LAUGH, EXCEL AND TRAVEL.

First published in 2018
by Lyssipos Press
United Kingdom
lyssipospress@gmail.com

Photography & Text
Hannisze

Editing
Debs Lloyd
Samantha Yong

Conception and Design
Peter Morley
Good Catch Design
Australia
www.goodcatch.com.au

Printed and bound in the United Kingdom
Deanprint Limited
www.deanprint.co.uk

ISBN : 978-1-9996084-0-8

ACKNOWLEDGEMENTS

I am forever grateful to my husband, **Argyrios Papathanasopoulos**, without whom I would not have captured any of the images in this book. Not only is he my perfect soulmate in life, he is also the one who is instrumental in helping me recognise the ability I do not myself know I possess.

My heartfelt thanks and appreciation to the following people, who have contributed in their own special ways, in bringing this book to life:

Linda Dabley, the appreciative friend who has first put the idea of making my own book into my cluttered head:
"When are you going to produce a book of travel photography with all these insightful extracts that you write?"

Dirk Liebich, the persistent friend whose overwhelming encouragement and confidence in my skills, reignited the idea of the making of this book:
"You must make a book. I am serious. Think big! Like in BIG. These photographs are phenomenal and deserve an audience."

Mel Winder, the supportive friend who made me believe that there are people who may be interested in buying my book if I make one:
"Dying to set my hands on a book of your amazing photos and adventures that you have had over the past years, of people and places you have been to. You are so talented!"

Enrique Stavrakopoulos, the honest friend who has provided me with his insightful feedback and critical opinion, although sometimes he can be remarkably forthright:
"What? You can't make a book in that size! No one's going to buy it. Listen – this book is an investment, not something people will read in the toilet. I want to put it on my coffee table, you know?"

Peter Morley, the talented Book Designer who helped me to conceptualise and shape this book from start to finish. I had never imagined so much is involved in the making of a book. All through the process, he has guided me with grace and patience.

Debs Lloyd, the gracious friend, an author in her own right, who read through my draft in its early stage, amended the errors, and suggested great alternatives to improve on my storytelling in a language which is not my mother tongue.

Samantha Yong, the meticulous niece who painstakingly combed through my final draft, and detected every missing alphabet and punctuation mark in it. She also made me realise that I love repeating myself.

My siblings - **Albert, Agnes and Alice**, and **Uncle Keong**, who have supported me through prayers and financial means, and made me who I am today.

To take photographs means to recognize – simultaneously and within a fraction of a second – both the fact itself and the rigorous organization of visually perceived forms that give it meaning. It is putting one's head, one's eye and one's heart on the same axis.

HENRI CARTIER-BRESSON

I am not a professional photographer and by that, I mean photography is not my paid occupation. It is my passion.

I grew up in a family who relied on photography as a source of income. My late parents owned a photography shop in a rural town in Malaysia. My father would travel to villages to take photographs of people, and developed the film himself in a little darkroom at the back of our shop. As soon as I was able to sit on my own, I was allowed to accompany him while he worked in this "Magic Room".

I remember feeling absolutely fascinated when faces miraculously appeared on the pieces of paper my father had soaked in some foul-smelling chemical. He, in turn, took pleasure in my pure delight and thousands of questions.

As one who was brought up in such an environment, you might say that photography is in my blood.

I hold a degree in Law and Music from a British university, and I have practised as an Advocate and Solicitor for 16 years in Malaysia, before ceasing work and moving to England. My husband and I currently reside in a scenic little village in West Yorkshire, one of the most beautiful parts of the country.

Having been trained extensively to have an analytical mind in both the mediums I had studied, it has subconsciously become ingrained in my personality. It is a trait I often use in my photography.

Although many of the images here may seem to have been captured spontaneously, in actual fact, a lot would have happened before they were taken. The quote above, by my favourite photographer, Henri Cartier-Bresson, sums it all up for me. In those few seconds before I clicked my camera, I would have used my head, my eyes and most importantly, my heart, in making decisions on how and when to freeze those crucial moments, before turning them into lasting memories.

This book showcases some of these memories and tells the "stories" behind the images I have captured over the years. I invite you to journey with me through my images.

There is nothing in this world which does not have a decisive moment, and the masterpiece of good ruling is to know and seize this moment.

JEAN FRANÇOIS PAUL DE GONDI, Cardinal de Retz

ETHIOPIA

We were visiting a village belonging to the Hamar tribe, and as soon as we alighted from our car, a group of women and girls began to surround us, all wanting to pose for photographs in return for some money.

As I was looking to capture something more candid and authentic, I wandered away from them. My attention was drawn to a group of children nearby. I sat and watched them from afar, before inching forward and clicking my camera.

I love how tenderly the girl was looking at the boy, and the coy expression on the boy's face in response. This, to me, was *the* decisive moment of their interaction, and I am so pleased to have seized and frozen that precise moment in time.

*Kindness is the language which the deaf can hear
and the blind can see.*

MARK TWAIN

We met this little girl in a town called Hawzen, located in the Tigray region of Ethiopia, the northernmost of the country's nine regions, bordered by Eritrea to the north, and Sudan to the west.

We were visiting a local market, and being the only foreigners there, we attracted quite a bit of attention and ended up having a big group of children following us.

This girl was my constant companion that morning. We somehow managed to communicate without sharing a common language. I have always believed that kindness can be shown in many ways, and certainly not only by material means. Kindness in mannerisms will almost always be recognised and reciprocated by strangers, even children.

It was through kindness that I became friends with this girl. And when I raised my camera to photograph her, she gave me this look of trust.

"She helps me with all my chores." "How old is she?" "She will be four next month."

That was the conversation we had with this beautiful mother and daughter when we met them on the road in Ethiopia. Despite their strenuous task, they looked like they were having a fun day out. The little girl seemed to be wearing her best dress!

Seeing their cheerful smiles that day brought tears to my eyes. This image to me, truly epitomises the resilience of the Ethiopian people.

It is an established custom in the South Omo Valley for visitors to pay the tribes a small token of money in return for photographs taken of them. As we were leaving a Mursi village, these two girls came running after me and shouted, "Photo, Photo, Miss! Three Birr, one people." (*Yes, in English!!!*) When they sensed that I was reluctant (as I had already taken many photographs by then), the one in blue said, "Three Birr, two people," pointing to herself and the little one. I laughed at her persistence and when I agreed, they stood to attention and looked straight into my camera.

When I handed out six Birr to them instead of the three Birr they had asked for, they broke into smiles and thanked me. Whenever I look at this image, I find myself replaying that interaction. It never fails to make me smile.

We were on the road when we met these two boys tending to a herd of cattle. They were not friendly initially, eyeing me with great caution, as I stepped out from the car.

I greeted them and started to communicate through gestures. I am a firm believer that it takes only a smile, to get one in return. It is, I think, the only universal gesture that can break all barriers. I put that into practice and managed to make them look this happy just before I clicked my camera.

I captured these beautiful Hamar girls just when a rainbow was forming behind them. They were humorous and feisty at the same time. After spending a few hours at the village with them, I found the younger girls to be more outspoken and independent compared to the older women, who were more gentle and submissive. When it came to posing for photographs, they were like supermodels – no directions or instructions from me were required.

Although the Ethiopians are generally very friendly people, I find the tribal men not to be so. They have somehow perfected the macho, serious look and demeanour to accompany the superior status accorded to them in their communities. I saw this man by the side of the road from our car. I was captivated by his colourful attire. We stopped and I asked if I could photograph him. He seemed very pleased with the request and agreed willingly. When I made a gesture for a smile, he generously accorded me with this beautiful grin. I do not have many images of tribal men with smiles, so this is really a treasure!

nother child in the family means another pair of hands to help out with the many chores around the household, no matter how young that child is. This is true in many parts of the world, including Ethiopia.

While many girls her age are treated like princesses and have not a single care in the world, this little one here is already carrying a whole load of burden on her young shoulders. I captured this image of her when she was trying to placate her howling sibling. I am sure she will grow up to be resilient and capable at overcoming adversities, like the many Ethiopian women whom we have met in the country.

I met this lady at a secluded part of a Hamar village. She was walking very slowly and stopped dead in her tracks when she saw me.

In the extreme heat, the red ochre applied to her hair has dripped down one side of her face, and her left eye looked infected. As I drew closer, she smiled, and there we were, smiling and looking at each other with mutual curiosity.

I pointed at my camera and gestured to ask for permission to photograph her. She responded with what I imagined to be a look of disbelief, straightened herself, and looked straight into my lens.

As I clicked my camera, the raging question I was longing to ask her was, "What is your story?"

→

While the Hamar women were gregarious and full of humour, the men maintained their distance and kept watch over all that was happening from afar.

We saw this group of men (and boys) when we were about to leave their village. To me, they appeared to be rather unapproachable. However, as we were walking towards our car, something inside me was screaming for a photograph of them. So, I turned around and walked back to the group, and simply asked the oldest member, "Photo?", while pointing at my camera.

This image was the result of a single (albeit very slight) nod from him.

We were born of love; Love is our mother.

R U M I

I have witnessed from our travels that in most parts of the world, there is no reliance on electrical gadgets or fancy toys to keep a child quiet, happy, smiling and contented. That it is possible to have a conversation with a child. That a child can be shaped from young with love and responsibilities. That the natural state of motherhood is unselfishness.

I thought a lot about this during our many encounters with the Ethiopian women, who were almost always seen together with their children. I observed the existence of an undeniable bond between the mothers and their children – one that was borne entirely out of love and not materialistic bribery.

The image of this beautiful lady and her child often brings me back to those thoughts. By the look of it, she has had a long and tiring day under the blazing sun, with the little child as her faithful companion. When I look at this photo, I not only see, but feel gentleness and love.

Beauty is in the eyes of the beholder, so they say. In the case of the Mursi tribe of Ethiopia, the wearing of a lip plate signifies such beauty, and is often worn by unmarried and newly married women in the tribe.

This lady was the quieter one among the women who had gathered around me. I observed the love she had shown towards her child - gently caressing and softly whispering into the baby's ears, when those around her were loud and raucous. That was the reason she stood out from the crowd for me. And that was why I chose to photograph her. However, no matter how hard I tried, I could not get her to smile.

L ike many things that are constantly changing and developing around the world, traditional practices within certain cultures are slowly becoming unpopular among the younger generation. When we were in Ethiopia, we saw many teenage Mursi girls of marriageable age and some newly married ones who choose not to have their lips pierced. This newly married lady was one of them. I admire her confidence, defiance and of course, her elaborate headgear and face-painting.

← The lip-plate worn by this Mursi lady is by far, the largest I have seen during our visit to Ethiopia. It looked really painful and uncomfortable to my unfamiliar eyes, but I could sense her pride in wearing it. She also has some delicate swirls of raised flesh on her right arm, and we were told that to create such a pattern, her skin would have been pulled with thorns and cut with razor. Patterns like these are considered a sign of beauty within the tribe, in addition to lip-plates.

→ We met this lady and her male companion when we were on the road in Ethiopia. She was not wearing any lip-plate although her lips were pierced. We were informed that this is quite normal in older married women (even if their husbands are still alive). Once their husbands die, the lip-plate is discarded and never to be worn again. She was a little hesitant to be photographed because she was not "dressed up". When I persisted, she finally relented.

←

We saw this lady and a few others by the side of the road. They looked like they were on the way to the market to sell their possessions.

When I approached to ask whether I could photograph her, she looked pleased that I had chosen her over some of the younger women in the group. She swiftly grabbed a cockerel from the hands of one of them, before standing attentively for me. I tried vey hard not to laugh out loud.

From beneath those beads covering her eyes, I would like to think that she was smiling into my lens.

→

Of all the tribes we visited in Ethiopia, I find the Hamar people to be the most colourful. They adorn themselves with intricate, colourful bead necklaces. While the boys are usually shirtless, the unmarried girls wear animal skin adorned with seashells and beads to cover their front. The children in this image were professionals when it came to posing for photographs. As soon as I raised my camera to my eye, they knew how to stand, look and smile. And they did it all so naturally. At times, they even suggested how they should pose!

A great photograph is one that fully expresses what one feels, in the deepest sense, about what is being photographed.

ANSEL ADAMS

I think it is not unfair to say that our future is largely determined by where we were born. This very thought is always on my mind when I witness the daily struggles of some of the people we meet during our travels. At times like these, I often wonder how differently their lives would turn out to be, if only they had been born in another country.

We met this lady and her child when we were on the road in Ethiopia. The lady looked exhausted and was carrying a big load of firewood, in addition to her child. We were told that they were still a long way from home.

I have to admit that I was greatly affected by this unexpected encounter. I took time to reflect on all our "urban" complaints, and realised how trivial they really were, in comparison with the difficulties faced by some of these less fortunate people. It is true what they say about travelling, that it changes your perspective on life.

From the metal-and-leather necklace and the two metal rings worn around her neck, you can tell that this lady is the first of her husband's three wives. According to the Hamar tradition, a man can have as many wives as he can afford, cattle-wise (the dowry to be paid in order to gain a wife).

We were told that the first wife is often viewed as the 'luckier' and more superior one, with the younger wives being treated more like slaves than wives. This image, in my opinion, seems to contradict this presumption. Looking at what she was carrying, it is safe to say that this lady has certainly been hard at work under the hot sun for a long duration. I wonder what her story is. I would really love to know.

As we were leaving a village belonging to the Dassanach tribe, a group of children and teenagers decided to accompany us to the river bank.

At one point during the long walk, I came up with an idea to create a little game with them. Through the interpretation of our guide, I asked them to stand in a row and jump as high up in the air as they could, for me to photograph them.

When I showed the images to them from my camera screen, they bent over with laughter and wanted to do it all over again, as some of them were blocked by the others in the images. So, we continued with our little game, until they were all satisfied.

This scene was one of the many which I captured that afternoon. Whenever I look at it, I can hear their joyful laughter echoing through the barren land.

Impromptu encounters with the locals always turn out to be the most memorable experiences in all our travels. The events leading up to these unexpected meetings often form the interesting part of the narratives to my images.

We met this couple when we were driving through a rural part of Ethiopia.

Although I did not understand what they said when we asked to photograph them; from their shocked reaction alone, I could guess that they were saying something to the effect of, "What? Here? With us looking like this?"

I laughed at their reaction, guided them to face me, and clicked my camera as quickly as possible, before they could change their minds.

This unbelievable scene was another of these unexpected encounters. I remember it vividly. We had been on an uneventful drive for hours when, out in the middle of nowhere, we saw these two guys scrambling up their poles by the side of the road ahead of us. The sight of them standing precariously on those high poles totally caught me by surprise, as that was the last thing I had expected to see. My initial shock soon turned to amusement, and we stepped out of the car to speak with them, before I photographed them against the beautiful blue sky.

←

We were told by this young man that he was on his way to the weekly market to sell the honey he had collected and kept in the containers on his shoulders.

I was very amused to see him wearing hair-clips. Despite their girly colours and feminine designs, those clips looked like they belonged there. He shyly obliged my request for a photograph.

Only Ethiopian men can carry off those hair-clips like he did, without looking ridiculous or unmanly. He still looks very masculine, don't you think?

→

Of all the tribes we visited in Ethiopia, the Dassanach is my favourite. I find them to be very good-natured and funny. As soon as we arrived at their village, which can only be reached by crossing the Omo River in a "canoe" crafted out from a tree trunk, we were greeted warmly by a group of women.

To attract us into photographing them (in exchange for a small token of money), they would position themselves strategically, as if they knew that a photographer can never resist a good composition. I fell into their "trap" willingly, and this image is the result of their impeccable business acumen.

←

These ladies were sitting in front of their igloo-shaped hut, appearing completely cool and perfectly poised. I stopped (they knew I would), and composed my framing visually before nodding to them (a signal that I wanted permission to click), lifted my camera to my eye, framed, waited for the child to reach for his milk, and clicked.

I love the look on their faces. There is a certain kind of overpowering strength in it. It is the kind of look that many people with material needs are lacking. This, to me, is a look which says, "I am very comfortable with myself. I am not impressed with what you have."

→

They were weaving leather strips (or pretending to be) when we met them. As soon as I raised my camera, they stopped weaving, looked straight at me, and waited to be photographed. I paused and turned to our guide for translation help. I asked him to tell them to continue weaving and not to look at me. I could guess their reaction when my request was conveyed. The older lady was saying something in an incredulous tone – probably asking the guide, why would I not want them to look at my camera, if I intend to photograph them?

I captured this just as she was looking up to our guide for an answer.

This lady was the shy one amongst the group of women who had gathered around me. I observed that while the others were pushing forward to get my attention, she was standing alone outside the circle and watching the ruckus from a safe distance.

I pushed through the crowd and walked towards her. I could see her withdrawing a little. She looked around with a hint of disbelief and somewhat embarrassed look, as if she was apologising to the others that I have chosen to photograph her and not them. I touched her upper arm and greeted her gently. She began to relax and we spoke through the translation of our guide.

I captured this after I felt that she was comfortable enough to be herself in my presence. I love her genuine smile. To me, it was not merely a smile from her lips, but one which emanated with warmth from her soul, heart and eyes.

Let my soul smile
through my heart
and my heart smile
through my eyes,
that I may scatter
rich smiles
in sad hearts.

PARAMAHANSA YOGANANDA

While some visitors to the tribal villages in Ethiopia may perceive the constant requests for photographs from the villagers as annoying harassment, we took it all in good stride and responded with humour.

These two girls were following me around their village, repeatedly asking me to photograph them. The first time I saw them, they were posing with some baskets in their hands, and when I did not respond, they were disappointed. Before long, they appeared ahead of me again, and this time, they were clinging affectionately to each other and calling out to me.

I could not help but laugh at their persistence. And this time, I clicked.

We met this family at a Mursi village we were visiting. The children clambered out from their hut as we walked past, curiosity written all over their faces. When I asked for permission to photograph them, they called out to their mother, who was inside the hut. A lady appeared at the entrance with a baby in her arms and much to my amusement, she said sheepishly, "Five Birr" (£0.13) while pointing to herself. She then pointed at her children and repeated, "Three Birr" (£0.08) after each one of them.

Everyone is handed adversity in life.
No one's journey is easy.
It's how we handle it
that makes people unique.

KEVIN CONROY

It was raining heavily. The road was muddy and the evening was turning cold. We met this group of resilient ladies who had been out the entire day, collecting firewood for their daily use. Despite the heavy weight of their load, they remained cheerful, facing the adversities in their lives in an applaudable manner.

I was determined to capture this scene despite the heavy rain. The ladies did not stop walking when I pointed my camera at them. As they continued taking their small painful steps, I continued clicking. I was so glad it was raining, because no one would realise that I was actually crying when I captured this scene.

This image humbled me. It is one of those images that speaks louder than words.

←

While we were waiting for our *'injera'* (sourdough-risen flatbread) and Ethiopian coffee to be served at a local eatery, this little one (the owner's daughter) came out from her house to look at us curiously.

My husband blew a balloon, but instead of giving it to her, he deflated the balloon on her face, causing her to break into a fit of laughter. She enjoyed the game so much and asked for it to be repeated a few times.

Whenever I look at this photograph, it reminds me of how little it takes to make a child happy.

→

Not far away from the eatery, there was a group of children playing outside their dilapidated wooden huts. We walked over to give them some balloons. They were surprised at this unexpected gesture, and when news got around that free balloons were being given, more children began to gather around us.

I captured the image of this adorable little boy as he was looking up expectantly at my husband, waiting for his balloon. I have intentionally included part of my husband's fingers in the frame to indicate his presence in the child's line of vision.

The little boy's immense joy at the prospect of receiving something so simple should serve as a reminder to all of us, that a child can be taught to be happy and contented, even with the simplest things.

It was in a village at Konso that we met these adorable girls. We were walking through their maze-like village with interesting tree-trunk boundaries and agricultural terraces, and they followed us. They were sweet-natured and very inquisitive, and when I communicated with them through gestures, they responded with laughter and smiles.

They looked curiously into my camera when I asked to photograph them. They did not smile initially, because they probably had no knowledge of what I was about to do. I had to make some funny faces and gestures to get this reaction. They probably thought I was quite mad!

The Tigray people from the northernmost region in Ethiopia, are known to have used face scarification for the expression of their cultural identity. When a child is about two to six-years old, two very small incisions in the shape of a cross will be made on the forehead. The cuts will be very thin and hardly noticeable if done properly. However, if the incisions are done by an unskilled person, they will become noticeable scars. We met this boy as he was walking back from school one afternoon. He was the first Tigraian I have seen with a "cross scar" on his forehead. I was fascinated by the sight of this unique mark.

To me there is no picture so beautiful
as smiling, bright-eyed, happy children;
no music so sweet as
their clear and ringing laughter.

P.T. BARNUM

We met this group of children when we were on the road in Lalibela. We stopped our car to greet them and to distribute some balloons we had brought with us. They were delighted with our simple gifts, and before long, shrieks of excitement echoed through the air as they jumped up and down, trying to catch the floating balloons.

Seeing the joy on their faces, I decided to create a little game to entertain them. Through the translation of our guide, I asked them to race towards me at the count of three. As I positioned myself away from them with my camera, my husband acted as the "race starter".

They were thrilled with the game. Whenever I look at this image, I find myself replaying the events leading up to the capture of this joyous scene. And I can still hear their ringing laughter from that memorable day.

We met this boy as we were descending the hill after visiting the Asheton Maryam Monastery in Lalibela. As we were on high ground, the weather was rather cold, which explains why the boy had wrapped a white cloth around himself. This manner of dressing is rather common among the pilgrims in the ancient city. He was rather shy when we came face-to-face, hiding his face even further under the wrap. We stopped to speak to him for a while, before I asked to photograph him. He nodded shyly and gave me a smile. I have intentionally not moved the white cloth covering his mouth, as I wanted to show his dazzling smile through his eyes. If you look very closely, you can see my reflection in his eyes.

It was in one of the rock-hewn churches in Lalibela that we met this lonely man. Seated in the shadows of the church to avoid the blistering heat outdoors, I almost missed him. He seemed to be in a world of his own, watching everything that went by expressionlessly.

I approached him slowly, pointed at my camera and then at him. I received no response. I stepped back, lifted the camera to my shoulder level and pointed at it again, and then at him, waiting for an answer. This time, he gave me a gentle nod – and nothing else. His poise remained stoic, as he looked into my lens in that same expressionless state as when I first saw him.

She had them all set up in an organised manner - similar designs were arranged to sit together – rooster with rooster, lion with lion, the taller ones were placed on the top, slowly cascading down in height, with the crosses and rings at the bottom and the shell ornaments on the right.

She then sat herself on a tiny piece of cloth on the dusty ground in that small enclosure she had claimed as her 'shop' for the day. And she waited – with a small hand-held fan and more crafts for her to work on, in her little canvas bag by her side. She had come well prepared for the blazing afternoon sun, but the one fact that she could not be certain of, was how many customers she was going to get by the end of that day.

Do you remember what you were doing when you were her age?

Whenever we travel to a new country, the one place that we never fail to visit is the local market. It is often there that we get the opportunity to mingle with the locals, eat with them and learn more about their daily lives.

It was at the textile section of the market in Lalibela that we met these boys. Their parents were nowhere to be seen, and they seemed to be manning the stall all by themselves. We chatted via gestures, before I pointed at my camera and asked whether I could photograph them. While the elder boy nodded and immediately straightened his posture with a ready half-smile, the little one became all shy and coy, hid his adorable face behind his brother, and stifled a giggle in the process.

M y gift of instant prints to the people I photograph has always been received with gratitude. The smiles elicited from the happy recipients by this simple gesture never fails to bring immense joy to me.

This man had never seen a photograph of himself before. He could not understand when I told him that his face would be visible on the small piece of instant film that I had just given him.

His initial puzzlement soon turned into delight when he saw his image appearing slowly before his eyes. A slight smile began to form on his lips, as his eyes attentively focused on the print.

To him, it was Magic. To us, it was Joy.

This young priest had been so used to broken promises by tourists who told him they would send photos they had taken of him, that he barely lifted a smile when I asked to photograph him.

He did not know then, that I was going to give him an instant print of himself. I had timed myself to capture his reaction at the precise moment he saw his image appearing on the print. This image of him with his gorgeous smile is the result of my patience.

I remember the American actor, Brad Garrett, once said : "You take away all the other luxuries in life, and if you can make someone smile and laugh, you have given the most special gift : Happiness." I would like to think that I have done at least that.

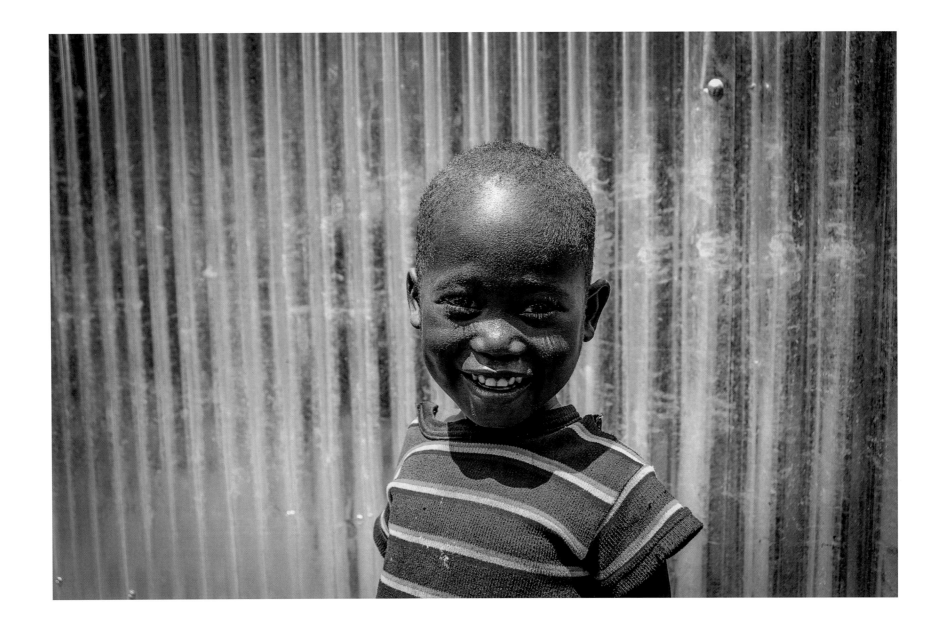

This little boy is from the Aari tribe of Ethiopia. When we walked around his village with our guide, he held on tightly to my hand as we strolled hand-in-hand like good friends.

I talked to him and asked him questions as we walked, and he would answer with a nod and a smile, as if he understood me. At one point, he exclaimed loudly and excitedly while pointing to a house nearby. Our guide turned around and said, "He is telling you that this is his house!"

When he noted that I had understood what he was trying to tell me, he beamed his electrifying smile at me. I positioned him against the zinc wall surrounding his house and pointed my camera at him.

This is the result of that click – right in front of his house.

We met this little girl in Konso. She was following us quietly as we explored her village. She did not respond much when spoken to, but seemed content to be just tagging along with us. I continued to talk as I walked beside her, and it was after she had warmed to me a little, that I managed to elicit this small smile from her.

I noticed that she had some faint marks of tattoo on her face, which were not done very well. I wonder why she was marked that way. No one seemed to know.

A good photograph is one that communicates a fact, touches the heart and leaves the viewer a changed person for having seen it. It is, in a word, effective.

IRVING PENN

MABUL ISLAND, MALAYSIA

I met this boy, his grandmother and younger sister in a fishing village at Mabul, a small island off the coast of East Malaysia. They were sitting on the landing of their stilt house to cool down from the scorching afternoon heat. I chatted with the grandmother for a while, before asking whether I could photograph them. As the boy turned to look at me, his state of discomfort from the oppressive heat was clearly obvious. I decided to focus solely on him and the beads of sweat dripping down his face.

As I wandered further into the village, I marvelled at the sight of the swaying coconut trees and listened to the sounds of waves lapping gently against the shore.

Before long, I saw many children, all gathered under the stilt houses for some shade against the strong afternoon sun. They approached me cautiously, until I began speaking to them in the Malaysian language. They looked at me in surprise, as if not expecting an Oriental-looking person to be speaking the same language as theirs.

And then they surrounded me, fighting over each other to ask me questions and to show me their simple handmade toys. As I responded to their chatter, I happened to look up and saw this sweet little face, looking down at me from her stilt house. My heart instantly melted as I reached for my camera.

At one end of the village, I saw this girl attending to some customers at a stall. When they left and she came into my full view, I noticed the melancholic look on her face. She was gazing at some girls who were playing boisterously nearby. I observed her from afar. When she finally realised my presence, she was a little embarrassed, as she discovered that I had been watching her. I raised my camera and asked, "Gambar?" *(Photo?)*

She was shy all of a sudden, leaning her body against the stall and wrapping her arms around herself. I waited to see whether she would refuse, but she looked straight into my camera and gave me this lovely smile.

I was surprised to see this little girl manning the stall all by herself. How will she manage the money transactions, I wondered?

After staying to watch for a while, I discovered that every time there was a customer, she would call out to her mother, who was busy with other chores at the back of the stall. I guess in some parts of the world, children are entrusted with duties and responsibilities much earlier in their lives.

I walked over to where she was and called out to her, "Adik!! Senyum." (*Little One!! Smile.*) And she responded by giving me this adorable smile.

As I walked through the dilapidated wooden houses scattered around the village, I felt a sudden wave of sadness enveloping me by the sight of such poverty. While I was still coming to terms with this reality, I felt a pair of eyes on me. That was when I saw him, looking down at me from his family's stilt house.

He looked like he had just been splashed with water. I called out to him in Malaysian, "Adik!! Apa khabar?" (*Little One!! How are you?*) Judging from the hesitant look on his face, I think he did not quite know how to respond to a stranger.

The face is the mirror of the mind,
and eyes without speaking
confess the secrets of the heart.

ST. JEROME

CUBA

I have always believed that you can tell what is on the mind of a person simply by looking at their faces, especially the eyes.

We met this man when we were strolling along the streets of Trinidad. He was sitting on the pavement outside a shop, singing and playing his guitar – with a little box in front of him, hoping for some loose change. Although he was singing and playing as if he was enjoying himself, the fact that he was doing it for money showed that he would have preferred to be doing something else which might "guarantee" some earnings in return, if he could.

One look at his face and my heart went out to him. To me, he has the kindest and most honest face – jovial, friendly, gentle and humble. Instead of just giving him some money and walking away, we sat with him on the pavement, clapped in appreciation when he finished, talked to him and requested a few Spanish songs, which he sang to us with enthusiasm. I am not sure how we made him feel that day, but he sure made our day!

We were walking along the famous and busiest street of Old Havana called Obispo when we saw this charismatic lady, sitting quietly against a yellow wall, all dressed up in her traditional Caribbean costume. She was smoking her cigar very slowly with a faraway look on her face.

Many tourists stopped to photograph her and I too, joined the queue and waited for my turn to capture her beautiful face. To me, she was the epitome of Cuban beauty – her dark eyes sparkling and lively, and her broad smile dazzling and enigmatic.

Old Havana is certainly charming and very unique. It is hard not to fall in love with this beautiful part of the city, despite all the pot holes on the streets and the crumbling structures surrounding the area. With electric wires dangling over our heads and zig-zagging across the once magnificent buildings, it was hard not to feel guilty when we stepped into the comfort and opulence of our hotel.

It was while we were exploring one of the little alleys that we saw this lady walking towards us. She was using a walking stick as she limped on, at a very slow pace. Both her legs were as thin as chopsticks and she looked extremely fragile to me.

When she saw us, she stopped dead in her tracks. We greeted her in Spanish before I asked to photograph her. She nodded her head and smiled.

←

I t is so easy to be transported back in time in Trinidad, one of Cuba's best preserved colonial towns. The colourful buildings lent a lively and artistic vibe to the city; the cobbled stone paths and horse carriages made me feel like I had just stepped into a classic cowboy movie set.

We met this man sitting on one of the walkways outside a restaurant. His eyes looked glazed – I am not sure whether it was due to cataracts or the effects of alcohol. He was mumbling to himself, and when I approached to ask him some questions, his answers were incomprehensible.

After chatting for a while, I asked to photograph him. He nodded and looked straight at me. This was taken right before he scrambled to snatch away a piece of chicken that a tourist had just given to his dog.

→

I t was hot and humid when we were in Trinidad. This friendly man walked up to us, trying to sell us straw hats and fans. When I asked how much the fan cost, he answered, "Un peso" *(One peso)*. I told him jokingly, "Un ventilador, un foto. Si?" *(One fan, one photo. Yes?)* He smiled and stood up straight for my camera.

The best experiences from our trip to Cuba have got to be all our unplanned encounters with the locals on the streets. I wish we had spent more time on the beautiful island.

We sometimes encounter people,
even perfect strangers, who begin to interest us
at first sight, somehow suddenly, all at once, before
a word has been spoken.

FYODOR DOSTOEVSKY

INDONESIA

The above quote sums up succinctly how I felt when I first laid my eyes on this man. We met him at the famous Tegalalang rice fields near Ubud, on the island of Bali. He was sitting forlornly by the side of a narrow path, with a faraway look in his eyes.

I stopped to ask for permission to photograph him and he gladly agreed. He did not smile initially - probably because he was shy, for after all, we were strangers. I decided to stop clicking and began speaking to him in Indonesian.

After he had warmed to me, I asked whether he could smile for a few more photographs, which he did. When I showed him the images from my camera screen, he started laughing and said, "Look! No teeth."

It was during those split seconds that I withdrew my camera and captured the image that I had been waiting for – the one of him laughing heartily, without any embarrassment or inhibition.

I stayed on to chat with him for quite a long time after that, and he told me all about his missing teeth.

When we were in Bali, we went to watch a Barong and Kris performance. The dance is essentially a play with dancing, singing, dialogue and a little bit of comedy thrown in.

This beautiful dancer was in one of the scenes. She came on stage to do the Legong, one of the more popular form of Balinese dances. It is a very refined dance characterised mainly by intricate finger movements, complicated footwork, and very expressive gestures with facial expressions (especially the eyes).

I wanted to capture her at the precise moment when she was exhibiting all these elements at the same time, to produce an image which encapsulates all the characteristics of the dance in just one frame. After sifting through all my images, this is my favourite.

Heavily made-up to enhance his stage presence, this man here was my favourite character in the Barong and Kris performance. He cracked jokes in broken English (for the benefit of the foreign audience) and pranced around the stage like an agile deer.

The Balinese men often wear flowers behind their ears (frangipanis being the favourite); not just the stage performers. Like all things in life, this caught my attention when I first arrived on the island, due to my unfamiliarity with such a sight.

I wanted to capture the essence of this lovely man's character in the play, one which will exude an instant sense of joy and happiness to those who view it. I chose this one, which I hope will bring a smile to your face.

Since we cannot change reality,
let us change the eyes which see reality.

NIKOS KAZANTZAKIS

Looming 2,799m above sea level, Gunung Ijen in Indonesia's eastern Java is a volcanic wonder from a geological point of view. The smoky atmosphere which billows around its crater is what attracts thousands of visitors to the site each year. While the smoke looks like steam, it is actually highly concentrated hydrogen sulphide and sulphur dioxide gases.

Since 1968, local miners have been capping these fumaroles and chanelling the gases through ceramic pipes down to barrels. Inside the pipe network, the sulphur condenses and drips into the barrels as a red, hot liquid. This will turn into rock-hard sulphur when it cools.

Every day, around 300 men will descend into the crater, under restrictive breathing conditions, to break the sulphur slabs with little or no protective gear at all. Witnessing their back-breaking task was an eye-opener for me. It brought about some serious moments of reflection, coupled with unavoidably emotional tears.

The descent to the bottom of the crater was not easy. The path was extremely narrow and the terrain was very steep. It was also very slippery, as it was made mainly of loose, tiny stones. Every time a miner came up our way, we quickly stepped aside to the very edge to make way for them. Being so close to them as they walked past, I could see every drop of their perspiration and every line of their veins.

Despite their laborious task, they were very receptive to my request for photographs, and would smile and wave when I lifted my camera to focus on them. I framed this miner against the backdrop of the treacherous terrain to and from the rim of the crater, to show the difficult ascent which he was about to make, with the heavy load of sulphur slabs on his shoulders.

I have to admit that I was hiding my tears behind the camera when I captured this. His graciousness humbled me.

We found this miner at the bottom of the crater, sitting next to the network of pipes which were spitting out liquid hot sulphur. A few other miners were also nearby, waiting for the sulphur to cool sufficiently, in order to be broken into slabs and then carried to the rim of the crater.

The surrounding air, being the centre of the condensation activity, was particularly singeing. The mask that I was wearing, although necessary, was rather suffocating. When I took it off momentarily to speak to this man, my throat and eyes felt "burnt", and I had to put it back on immediately.

I marvelled at how most of the miners could work without wearing any masks. When I asked this man, he told me that after so many years, they had become accustomed to it. And with that, he gave me this lovely smile.

Kindness in words creates confidence.
Kindness in thinking creates profoundness.
Kindness in giving creates love.

LAO TZU

LESOTHO

The above quote has been my mantra for as long as I can remember. When put into practice, it has never failed me. I use it frequently whenever we meet strangers during our travels. I find people to be more vulnerable and shy in some parts of the world than others. They can often withdraw when I try to approach, and when that happens, I try to use a lot of tact and discretion in my approach, to help make them feel more at ease with my presence.

Once this barrier of unfamiliarity is broken, they often lose their inhibitions and suspicions towards us. I always wait for that to happen before I click my camera.

We met these beautiful people when we were driving through remote parts of Lesotho. We communicated with them mainly through gestures, coupled with a lot of laughter. When I asked for permission to photograph them, they willingly agreed. I have never allowed language to be an obstacle to the making of memorable encounters like these.

Good things happen when you least expect them – so the saying goes. That was exactly what happened to us during our road trip in Lesotho. We have been driving for hours without seeing anyone on the road. All of a sudden, a convoy of honking vans appeared ahead of us, driving haphazardly on the deserted road, with colourful flags sticking out of their windows.

We thought we had stumbled upon a village wedding. A few miles down the road, however, we saw many people lining up by the side of the road. We parked our car and got out to see what was happening.

When we finally found someone who could speak English, he informed us that they were participating in a cultural parade. All of the participants were dressed in different costumes to represent the different tribes, areas of origin and occupation.

Being the only foreigners there, I could tell that they were as curious about us as we were about them. For a few minutes, we stood there watching them, and they, watching us. Eventually, I snapped out of the trance and told myself that if I kept staring and not do anything, I would miss my photo opportunities! So, I got to work – and these are some of the images I took during that *very* unexpected encounter.

I find the Basotho people to be very friendly and receptive to being photographed. I did not have to do much to elicit smiles from them.

To me, photography is the simultaneous recognition, in a fraction of a second, of the significance of an event as well as of a precise organization of forms which give that event its proper expression.

HENRI CARTIER-BRESSON

SRI LANKA

We visited a pre-school in a village near Ella. It was about mid-morning and the only teacher (with her two assistants) was in the midst of feeding the children their lunch. We were told that they never had any visitors before, and the children were dumb-struck by our presence. They were shy but curious at the same time, peeking at us from behind doors.

I captured this scene, looking into one of the rooms where they were 'hiding' from us. I could not believe my eyes when I "caught" them in these exact positions, with these precise expressions on their faces. There was just so much innocence. I clicked my camera as quickly as I could, and just as I had expected, within seconds, both their positions and expressions changed.

A

t the same pre-school, I was trying my best to coax this shy little girl to smile and look at my camera, but all she did was to roll her eyes away, looking everywhere except at me! I continued to wait patiently, clicking my camera just as she was looking up at her teacher, who had been assisting by trying to persuade her to look at me. I will never forget this girl's gorgeous eyes.

I

t was when we were descending the hundreds of steps from the Dambulla Cave Temple, that we met this lady. She was sitting on one of the steps, begging. Her terribly hunched back caused her trouble when trying to lift up her head to make eye-contact with those who were going up and down the steps. I felt a cloud of sadness enveloping me at the mere sight of her tiny, frail body.

I went nearer, and it was then that I realised that she had problems with her sight as well. She turned her head awkwardly to look at me with her "good" eye and was probably a little surprised why I had approached her and squatted down to her level. I smiled and handed her some money, instead of placing it on her begging bowl.

When she felt that it was a note and not a coin, a small smile began to form on her lips. She slowly raised the note to her "good" eye to have a better look at it. I am pleased to have captured that smile on her face, but to this day, I am still left wondering, "Why was she there?" "Where was her family?"

Every time you smile at someone,
it is an action of love, a gift to that person,
a beautiful thing.

MOTHER TERESA

INDIA

As we walked along the many ghats by the Ganges River in Varanasi, we came face-to-face with this lady. She looked frail and was supporting herself with a sturdy stick as she walked very slowly amongst the crowd. We were approaching each other but when she saw me, she stopped and stood very still, and I realised that she was staring at me. I smiled and continued walking towards her.

When I came nearer to her, I put my hands together in front of my chest, bowed a little and said "Namaste". Her eyes twinkled and her lips lifted to form a smile, a very gentle one. Under those heavy wrinkles, I saw beauty, life, and of course, a thousand stories...

One day when we were in Varanasi, we decided to explore the city by foot and walked away from the riverfront. We walked through a maze of very narrow footpaths in between the cramped dwellings, most of which were devoid of any furniture, with only a roof over a limited space for the people to sleep in. Some were even sharing their indoor space with their cows/goats.

In the midst of the deafening noise and chaos, I noticed this little boy sitting all alone on the steps by the side of the path. He looked so forlorn and my heart went out to him.

As I approached and sat beside him, he began to recoil in fear. I took out a notepad and some coloured pencils and gave them to him. He looked at me blankly, and only then did it occur to me that he might not know what to do with them. I held his hand in mine and guided him to draw, just as I was taught when I was a child.

And then a miracle happened. He smiled. Not just a slight smile, but a wide toothy (well, in his case, toothless) grin. To me, that was a miracle, considering how sad and scared he had looked when I first met him, and how long it had taken him to warm to me. Whenever I look at this image, I feel immeasurable joy.

We decided to stroll along the Ganges River by foot early one morning to avoid the crowd and heat. As the first ray of sunshine began to turn golden, we came face-to-face with this girl on an almost deserted pavement. She was collecting empty plastic bottles to sell. I smiled and greeted her, using gestures and smiles to communicate. After a while, I said, "Photo?", and pointed at my camera. All of a sudden, she straightened up and stood to attention. The reverent cow at the background was just a lucky coincidence!

After showing her the images I had captured of her from my camera screen, I gave her some coloured pens and a notebook as gifts. She was grateful and could not stop smiling.

I photographed her again, as she sat on one of the steps, scribbling with the pens. I noticed that animals seemed to be drawn to her very naturally. The goat in the image had sauntered up to her; snuggling against her knees as she sat herself down on the step. I was quite sure this animal was not her pet, as they were not together when we first met her, but I might be wrong. I could not forget the smile on her face for the longest time after our brief encounter. It took so little to make her happy.

Out of the crowd in the midst of the morning chaos in Varanasi, I picked this man to photograph. He stood out from the others because he was very purposeful in his actions. He descended the steps, waded confidently into the river, lifted his face towards the rising sun and closed his eyes momentarily.

He then filled a container, held it up ceremoniously towards the golden sunlight with both hands, pausing to say a long prayer before tipping it over gently. Water began to drip rhythmically from the container, sparkling against the sunlight like gleaming jewels. As soon as it touched the surface of the river, circles of ripples began to form, creating a dazzling display of art strokes on the sacred Ganges.

Bewitched by the whole scene, I am surprised my finger found the shutter-button before the magic ended.

My favourite part of the day in Varanasi has to be the morning – very early in the morning. There is a certain eeriness in the calm and quietness of that time.

We saw this couple descending the steps and slowly submerging themselves in the murky river. As if guided by an invisible conductor, they lifted their hands simultaneously and pressed them together in front of their chests. They then gazed sombrely ahead at the rising sun, lost in thought.

I was so entranced by their synchronised movements that I nearly did not click my camera.

There are no facts, only interpretations.

FRIEDRICH NIETZSCHE

We had stopped to rest and were chatting to a *sadhu* (holy man), who had a limited command of English. While we were in the midst of our conversation, I saw this man stirring from his afternoon nap, and looking up at us. I waved at him, smiled, and descended the steps to sit next to him. After the usual greetings, I gestured to ask whether I could photograph him. He nodded and opened his right-hand palm, a symbolic gesture often used by *sadhus* when offering benediction to devotees.

Although he was clad in the saffron-clothing normally worn by *sadhus*, something in his eyes and demeanour told me that he was not actually a real or serious one. His kind face, however, carried a sad story, and it moved me to the extent that I was willing to let him believe that I believed what he wanted me to believe.

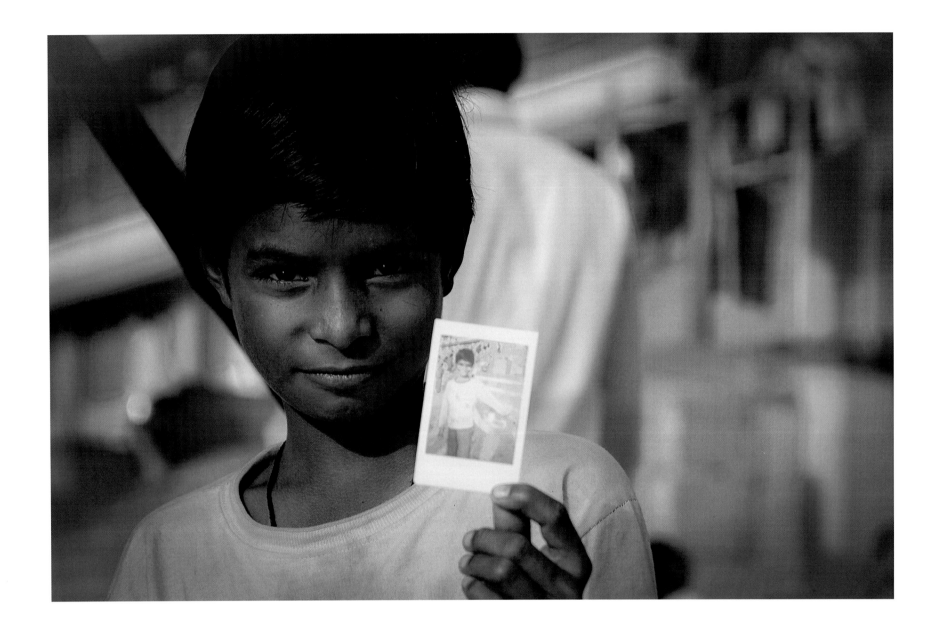

Whenever we travel, I like to bring little things with us as gifts - things that will delight the people we meet, especially the children. Not wanting to encourage the culture of begging, I usually source items which facilitate interaction.

One of the gifts that has proven to be a hit with all the recipients is the print taken with my instant camera. It never fails to bring a big smile to the recipient.

We met this boy when he was busy selling prayer candles and flowers by the Ganges River in Varanasi. After buying from him, we stayed to chat and I offered to take a photograph of him with my instant camera. He was overjoyed when he saw his image appearing on the film and proudly stuck the photograph among the candles and flowers in his basket for all to see!

I captured the image of this beautiful lady when we were being rowed in a boat on the Ganges River in Varanasi. She was seeing off a group of people who had just got into a boat. When I realised that I could capture her alone within the framing of my composition, it felt like I have stumbled upon a golden opportunity, for that is a rather unusual occurrence in a crowded place like Varanasi.

I did not realise then, how striking the colours of her blue blouse and red saree were, until after I had clicked my camera. Within seconds after I captured this, a group of devotees had descended the stairs and were standing right beside her, waiting for the next boat.

Photography is a way of feeling, of touching, of loving. What you have caught on film is captured forever... It remembers little things, long after you have forgotten everything.

AARON SISKIND

We were stuck in the usual heavy traffic while on the road to Agra when our car stopped next to a small van ferrying a group of children back from school. I could see many sweet faces peeking out from the side window.

I wound down our car window and waved at them. The little boy saw me first. He was not sure how to react initially. He looked up to the girl for guidance, and when he saw that she was smiling at me, he smiled too, as if to say, "Hey, look! That lady there is taking our photograph!"

Whenever I look at this image, I often wonder, what happened to his bandaged finger.

No act of kindness, no matter how small,
is ever wasted.

AESOP

It was at the famous stepwell of Chand Baori in Abhaneri (near Jaipur) that we met this lovely lady. She approached us as soon as we entered the site, with her little son tagging behind her. She spoke very little English, but the fact that she had tried to learn the language, in her attempt to communicate with tourists like us, impressed me. When we responded to her presence positively, I could sense her anxiety and hesitation dissipating.

She was soon "guiding" us around the complex, with her son holding on to my hand. We started asking questions about her and her family, and you could see a smile forming on her wrinkly face, as if she was surprised that there are people interested in knowing about her.

I asked to photograph her against the famous building leading to the stepwell. She nodded and straightened her body, and gave me a slight smile.

Dotted with lavish, magnificent palaces and surrounded by majestic hilltop forts, the beauty and elegance of Jaipur is undoubtedly evident. The opulence of all these monuments and complexes, however, paints a stark contrast between the extravagance of the past royalties and the simplicity (and depravation, in some cases) of the ordinary city dwellers.

I saw this lady after we had just visited the grand City Palace complex, and was immediately captivated by the colourful contrast of her attire against the yellow wall behind her. Her attention was drawn to a commotion nearby, and I photographed this just as she had turned her face to look at the people causing it.

I am pleased to have captured not only her curiosity, but also the plainness of her surroundings, which is a truer representation of the city.

As we explored the city of Jaipur by rickshaw, we moved past many traders who had spread out their myriad of wares for sale on both sides of the road, some of them just inches away from the crazy traffic. After a while, we decided to continue our exploration by foot.

It was in one of the many back alleys that we met these boys. The elder one was carrying a canvas sack, to be filled with recyclable materials which they had set out to collect, and to be sold later for a mere few coins. They stopped to pose for me when I asked to photograph them.

I was extremely touched to see the mutual adoration they have for each other. It broke my heart to know and see what they had to do, in order to feed themselves.

Childhood means simplicity.
Look at the world with the child's eyes –
it is very beautiful.

KAILASH SATYARTHI

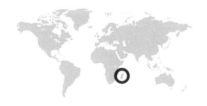

MADAGASCAR

We were on the road for a long time from Morondava heading north towards a village called Bekopaka. At one point during our journey, we had a flat tyre. So, we got down from the car while the driver and guide attended to the puncture.

We were stranded at a very remote part of Madagascar, where there were no proper roads to drive on. I doubt the villagers here have seen many vehicles passing through, let alone foreigners walking on their grounds. Groups of children began to gather around us to find out what was happening. Needless to say, our presence was received with apprehension by some, and curiosity by the others. I started making conversation with this group before photographing them. As you can see, each of them responded to me differently.

Whenever I look at this image, it always brings me back to that moment when we stayed and watched them play in a muddy river nearby. There were no fancy toys or gadgets. They only had one another and wild nature as their playground. Such simplicity. And yet, so much happiness.

We had gone to Madagascar in full anticipation of seeing the country's endemic animals and plants, in addition to climbing its incredibly sharp and mighty limestone formations known as Tsingy. We managed to accomplish all that without much difficulty.

What we had not anticipated, however, was to be totally enamoured by its people. Although the majority of them lived in extreme poverty, they were some of the happiest people we have ever encountered in all our travels.

We met this beautiful little girl as we were exploring a village in Bekopaka. She was on her way home after collecting firewood for the use of cooking. She looked so tiny in comparison to the weight of the load on her head. Despite her arduous task, she gave me this dazzling smile when I asked to photograph her. How can one's heart not be broken by such a sight?

$\rightarrow$

It was at a beach in the coastal town of Morondava that I met these two sisters. They looked like they have just returned from the market, judging from the provisions they were carrying.

"Salama" *(Hello)*, I greeted them in the Malagasy language. While the older sister was curious with my camera, the little one was a bit shy. I did not know how to say "Smile" in Malagasy, so I did a gesture of pulling both sides of my mouth upwards to try to get them to smile. This was their response.

It's not how much we have,
but how much we enjoy,
that makes happiness.

CHARLES SPURGEON

It was early in the evening, and we were exploring the centre of Morondava town on foot, visiting its market and shops. We did not want to leave because the town was so full of life. Like us, the locals were strolling the streets, taking advantage of the cooler temperature and the fading light of the day.

We met this group of boys as we walked along one of the alleys. They were entertaining themselves with some self-invented games, and we stayed to watch. They had created a sort of "competition" amongst themselves, to see who could do the highest jump from a hill of sandy stone.

I captured this just as they were leaping from the heap, with the youngest boy in the group still in a state of hesitation. The joy and happiness I witnessed in Madagascar remains one of the highlights of our many travels around the world. The Malagasy people remind me time and again, that we do not need to have much to be happy.

On our way back to our guesthouse after visiting the famous Andasibe-Mantadia National Park, we stopped at a village to buy some fruits. The village was full of life, as we were there at a time when the children had just finished school.

We met these two boys at a covered market and they were playing a game of marbles, right there, in between the stalls. After observing them for a while, I called out to them and asked if I could photograph them. Without direction, they automatically gave me this pose, as if they had done it many times before.

At the same village in Andasibe, I made eye-contact with this butcher, as he sat in his small stall, looking out at the passersby. I gave him a nod and a smile, before pointing first at my camera and then at him. He nodded in return, and was probably deciding how much of a smile to give me, when I clicked to capture this image of him.

Although his smile was indecisive, I am pleased with the approving look he offered me through his eyes. I could sense them smiling at me, amidst the hanging intestines and freshly cut-meat!

Above all, I craved to seize the whole essence, in the confines of one single photograph, of some situation that was in the process of unrolling itself before my eyes.

HENRI CARTIER-BRESSON

I met these children when they were having fun by the shore of Morondava Beach. Their happiness and joy were infectious. I attempted to communicate with them through gestures. They were very responsive and playful, and when I asked to photograph them, they grouped together on an abandoned boat and posed for me.

After every few clicks, they would crowd around me and asked to look at the images from my camera screen. They pointed at one another and burst out in laughter at the sight of themselves. Using only gestures, I then asked them to group together and run towards me.

This was one of the few images I took after that. Whenever I look at this image, I am transported back to that morning when I witnessed their mischievous behaviour and carefree laughter.

After crossing the Tsiribihina River on a "ferry" (basically planks of wood put and tied together), we reached a place called Belo Sur Tsiribihina, where we met these children playing on the dirt compound in front of their dilapidated wooden house.

I find them to be extremely gentle and vulnerable. I captured this after they had warmed to me, and when I showed them the images from the camera screen, they looked at me in amazement and giggled shyly.

It breaks my heart every time I look at this photo. Somehow, these children looked extremely fragile to me, and I can feel their eyes piercing right through my heart. Only a few images can give me such emotional effect.

These boys were racing against each other, up and down along a narrow lane when we met them. I thought the race was a bit unfair for the little one in blue, because the other two were much older than him. So, I stepped in and interfered. I placed them together at the start line, before leading the little one about 10 meters ahead of the other two. Once they understood what I meant, they were game for it, and were delighted when I placed my husband about 100 meters ahead, to "declare" the winner. We repeated the "race" a few times, and many other children soon came to join in the fun. The joy I feel when I look at this image is indescribable – and it proves to me time and again, that the greatest gift one can give to a child is time and love, not material things.

You don't take a photograph, you make it.

PERU

When I was travelling solo in Peru a few years ago, I took the Inka Express Bus from Cuzco to Puno. The bus stopped at several historical sites along the way to allow passengers to visit the attractions. It was at a place called Raqchi that I met this lady. I found her mumbling to herself, as she sat against a stone wall. I approached to ask whether I could photograph her. She stood up for this purpose, but did not smile in the first few photographs. She had a faraway look in her eyes and was not very responsive to my efforts in communicating with her.

After a while, I decided to make a final try to elicit a smile from her. The words that succeeded in bringing about this small smile: "Mira mi, señorita!" *(Look at me, young lady!)*

I met this little girl at La Raya, another one of the locations where the bus had stopped on my way to Puno. She was struggling to get her llama to move. Despite her attempt at pulling the rope which was tied around the llama's neck, the stubborn animal refused to budge.

It was quite a comical spectacle. I approached to speak to her and, when asked, she told me that the name of her pet llama was Lucy. She agreed to be photographed, but try as I did, I could neither get her to smile nor Lucy to look at me.

On my return trip from Puno to Cuzco, I decided to take an alternative mode of transportation to enable me to get a different view. I chose the luxurious Andean Explorer train, and ended up experiencing a spectacular journey in carriages which were adorned with subtle elegance from a bygone era.

The train stopped at La Raya (the highest point of the journey), where I had last met Lucy the llama and her owner. I got down to stretch my legs and met this beautiful lady and her daughter outside one of the souvenir stalls by the railway track. I approached them and after the usual greetings, offered a bun to the child. You can see how happy the child was, crumbs on her tiny mouth, and the bun in her tiny hand!

While in Puno, I took a boat to visit Lake Titicaca, the highest navigable lake (3,812m) in the world. We stopped at a very hilly island called Taquile, and it was here that I met this little boy. I was almost out-of-breath after a 20-minute vertical hike to reach the main square of the island, and had collapsed next to him, gasping for oxygen. I only realised his presence when my breathing finally became regular again. He was looking at me like this, as in this image.

After spending time talking to him, giving him balloons and making funny faces at him, I still could not get him to smile. Despite his lack of response, I photographed him anyway, because I found him simply irresistible!

When travelling, more often than not we are blessed with meeting happy faces who respond positively to our attempts at interaction.

In Peru, however, I saw many sad faces who looked like they were hardened by their difficult lives, even amongst the children. It was really heartbreaking at times, and it did make me feel very guilty to think that I was travelling for leisure, while they were struggling to survive.

I captured the image of this boy as he looked up at me from the rail tracks; his mother busily selling handicrafts to fellow train passengers. This, to me, is a look that can bring tears to the eyes.

It's one thing to make a picture of what a person looks like, it's another thing to make a portrait of who they are.

PAUL CAPONIGRO

I met this beautiful lady in Raqchi, after having visited some archaeological sites. She was one of the many locals who had set up stalls at the main square, selling handicrafts and souvenirs. Her face lit up when I approached her. In a very courteous manner, she showed me some of the items on sale, and described what they were made of. I was really touched by her soft-spoken voice. After buying a few items from her, I asked whether I could photograph her. She could not believe that of all the people around the square, I wanted to capture an image of her. In my broken Spanish, I told her, it was because she is beautiful.

This image, to me, encapsulates her gentle demeanour.

There are those who give with joy,
and joy is their reward.

KHALIL GIBRAN

BHUTAN

As with all our travels to the more remote parts of the world, I had brought along my instant camera to Bhutan, with the intention to spread some love and joy to the people we encountered.

We met these adorable monks at a monastery called Phajoding, and they were very surprised to see their images appearing gradually on the instant films that we had given them. From the look on their faces, I would like to think that we had brought some happiness and excitement to their lives during our brief encounter with them.

I found out much later that they had gathered all the instant photos and pasted them side-by-side in a scrap book. This happy image of them never fails to bring a smile to my face and tremendous joy to my heart.

Phajoding Monastery is one of the oldest and poorest monasteries in Bhutan. Situated at an elevation of 3,605m, life is harsh for the monks; the temperature is always low and the ground is often covered in snow during winter. We had the rare opportunity of spending a night there during our visit to the kingdom.

The man in this image is Lama Namgay Tenzin, the Principal of the monastery. It was due to his tireless efforts and determination that Phajoding is now a refuge and place of belonging for the young monks who live there, all of them underprivileged boys from impoverished backgrounds. I am so pleased to have photographed him in such a jovial mood.

Despite having to live with the simplest and most basic of necessities, the young monks at Phajoding Monastery were in high spirits when they met us. They were very friendly and enthusiastic to practise their English with us.

Of all the monks whom I interacted with, the one in this image was the shyest of them all. While the others approached me and asked for their photographs to be taken, this particular one was always standing at the back, silently observing all the chaos.

When I was busy entertaining the many requests for photographs, I happened to turn around to find him watching me in this exact pose. As I raised my camera to focus on him, he remained nonchalant, although he knew I was about to photograph him.

This image is one of my favourites – he looks like he was dreaming of something, lost in thought.

←

I was busy snapping and giving away instant photographs to the young monks when I felt someone pulling at the sleeves of my raincoat. I turned and saw this little one, who asked me to take a photo of him alone. He indicated that he wanted one taken of him sitting on some ancient steps.

I did not direct him to pose like this. He positioned himself on the steps, placed both hands on his bended knees, and crossed his little feet the way he did. The other monks said something to him, and he answered back. It went on for a while and I waited.

When all was silent, he nodded at me to indicate that he was ready. And I clicked, as instructed by the "little boss".

→

I met them on the grounds of Phajoding Monastery. We started chatting, as they both spoke basic English, which is one of the secular subjects (besides Maths) being taught at the monastery.

The one who was eating the instant noodles was very polite and generous, as he held out the packet and offered me some of his tasty snack. I took some from him and asked whether I could photograph them. They willingly agreed.

We had such a great time interacting with the young monks at the monastery. I witnessed many positive attributes in them - resilience, obedience, discipline, politeness. All the qualities that are essential in the making of a better human being.

Photography is an immediate reaction,
drawing is a meditation.

HENRI CARTIER-BRESSON

I was photographing a 6-day ultramarathon race in Bhutan (*The Last Secret* by GlobalLimits) and on one of the nights, we camped on the pristine grounds of the Chorten Nyingpo Monastery, said to have originally been built in 1587.

The runners were just settling down in their tents when I saw this curious monk observing their antics from afar. Judging from his expression, he must have seen something strange or new to his eyes.

I picked up my camera as soon as I could and captured his confused look without him realising. I am so pleased I managed to freeze this priceless expression in time, because as soon as I pressed my shutter-button, it vanished from his face. Like they say, timing is everything in photography.

Travelling leaves you speechless, then turns you into a storyteller.

MUHAMMAD IBN BATTUTA

MEXICO

Up in the treacherous mountain terrains of one of the most remote parts of the world, the Cooper Canyon in North Western Mexico, live the reclusive Indian tribe who call themselves Raramuri, or Tarahumara, to the rest of the world.

Since 2002, every year in the month of March, they descend from their dwellings to the little town of Urique for an ultrarunning race called the Ultra Caballo Blanco, created by the late Micah True. Named 'Caballo Blanco' (White Horse) by the tribe, Micah True was an American runner who had spent several years living and running with them.

It was this event which drew us to Urique a few years ago. I captured this scene just as many of the Raramuri people were coming into town. Some had walked for days to run in the race, as every participant will be given vouchers to exchange for food, which they so desperately need.

I will remember this sight forever, when we first saw a burst of amazing colours emerging before our eyes, out in the middle of nowhere. It was such a sight to behold.

As we mingled with the Raramuri people in the main square of Urique, we began our attempt at communicating with them. Since only a handful of them spoke Spanish, a lot of smiles and hand gestures were used in our interaction. I found them to be extremely shy, and it took quite some time for them to feel comfortable enough to look at my camera.

I approached this girl and her grandmother outside a shop. Judging from their tired looks, they must have walked for hours, if not days, to reach Urique. Their sad eyes pierced straight into my heart as I captured this.

Of all the tribes we have met during our many travels around the world, I find the Raramuri people to be the gentlest of them all. I have the impression that if faced with aggressive confrontation, they most likely will recoil and run, rather than stay and retaliate. Perhaps that was how they get their name, "Raramuri", which means The Running People.

We met this young couple as they were resting and having a snack, having just arrived in Urique on foot. They were wearing sandals made from tyre-tread and leather strips, which are commonly worn by almost all the Raramuri people. It is hard to imagine how they can move comfortably in them, on the unforgiving mountainous terrains which they call home.

Besides their clothes and basic farming tools, the people from this tribe have almost next to nothing. They are not used to interacting with outsiders due to their preference to hide away in the mountains, mostly for safety reasons and especially to avoid confrontation with the local drug cartels that have taken over the majority of their ancestral land by force.

Given such circumstances, it is not difficult to understand why they were so shy and reserved when we met them. It was not easy for me to extract a smile, even a very small one, from these ladies. It has taken us a few days to befriend them and to gain their trust. Despite their poverty and difficult lives, these beautiful people are gentle and resilient. It is as if they have accepted the fact that there is nothing much they can do to change their circumstances. So, they just soldier on, for the sake of their children.

That, to me, is a most admirable trait and a really hard act to follow.

These girls were trying to catch up with their mother, who had walked ahead of them.

I called out to them, "Hola! ¿Foto?" *(Hello! Photo?)*. As you can see, while the elder sister very willingly obliged me with her sweet smile, the younger one was not so pleased and was scowling at me without any hesitation. I love her expression though – it reminds me of what my mother used to tell me, "Don't talk or smile at strangers!"

It was at the Raramuri Indian Girls Boarding School (founded in 1941 by a visiting Jesuit priest) that I met this girl. The school is run by a group of nuns and teachers with the main intention of improving the living and learning environment of the local Raramuri girls who live near a town called Cerocahui, about 38km from Urique.

"Kuira" *(Hello)*, I said to her, in the Raramuri language. Switching to Spanish, I then asked her, "¿Como te llamas?" *(What is your name?)* She ran behind the pillar and checked me out with one eye peering and the other, hidden. "¿Foto?" *(Photo?)*, I persisted. She stepped out from behind the pillar when she saw my camera. That was when things began to get smoother between us.

Without the streets or dusks of Buenos Aires,
a tango cannot be written.

JORGE LUIS BORGES

ARGENTINA

When we visited the famous Sunday market at San Telmo in Buenos Aires, the atmosphere was electrifying. Pulsating music filled the air while the crowd strolled in mechanically-timed pace. No one was in a rush; everyone was just soaking up the intoxicating vibes in their own rhythm.

In the central square, a guy began to sing and strum his guitar, and this couple got up to dance. It was amazing to see how they glided across the pavement so smoothly and harmoniously. They were so in sync with each another.

I was totally mesmerised by their moves and their facial expression captivated me immensely. To this day, this photograph remains one of my favourites. For me, it exudes passion with a capital P!

Walking along the cobblestone streets of San Telmo, we met this man who called himself Gardelito, because he is an impersonator of the late Carlos Gardel, a well-known French Argentine singer. On the wall behind him, many of his photographs were displayed, and if you look closely, there is also one of the great Gardel himself. I was amused by the sight of him standing on a little box to make himself appear taller. I photographed him from a distance away because I wanted to capture that. When he realised I was photographing him, he made an angry face at me on purpose. Immediately after capturing this, he laughed and asked me to take another one, this time with him smiling. I prefer this image, because it shows the comical side of him.